Venture Begins

The Founder's Guide to Technical Requirements

Ship better software faster, maximize development ROI, and scale your business with confidence

979-8-9988477-0-7
979-8-9988477-1-4

Book Cover & Design by RH Publishing

First edition 2025

Contents

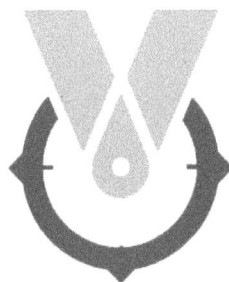

This is Not "Just Another Guide"

This is a straightforward guide. I'm not going to waste your time with fluff or theory. But before we begin, understand something important: don't take advice about building software from someone who hasn't (a) successfully built products that scale and (b) helped founders navigate technical challenges without a technical background.

I discovered this the hard way. Despite having success as a product manager at renowned companies, I found myself struggling to communicate the complex world of software development to founders who had brilliant ideas but couldn't speak "tech." The communication gap was costing them time, money, and in some cases, their entire business.

As you build your software product, you'll face critical decisions about what to prioritize, how to communicate with developers, and where to invest your limited resources. These decisions will either create a solid foundation for growth or trap you in a cycle of constant rework, technical debt, and missed deadlines.

Think of it like trying to build a house without speaking the language of architecture. Could you figure it out through trial and error? Maybe. But why spend your precious runway learning painful lessons when the blueprint for success already exists?

If your development team stopped understanding your vision today, would your product still match what your customers need tomorrow? For most founders without technical backgrounds, the answer is no.

I can't build your software for you, but I can show you how to transform your vision into clear technical requirements that developers can execute flawlessly. I've helped dozens of founders make this transition, bridging the gap between business goals and technical implementation.

Here's what you need to know: the journey from idea to successful software product doesn't have to be filled with expensive mistakes and miscommunications. Everything in this guide is about breaking free from the traditional founder-developer disconnect and giving you the tools to lead your technical team with confidence—even if you've never written a line of code.

Overview

This comprehensive template helps founders without a technical background clearly communicate feature requirements to development teams. This structured approach will reduce misunderstandings, improve development efficiency, and ensure the final product matches your vision.

There is a ton that goes into developing a software product. Here is a high-level overview of the stages and what occurs at each stage:

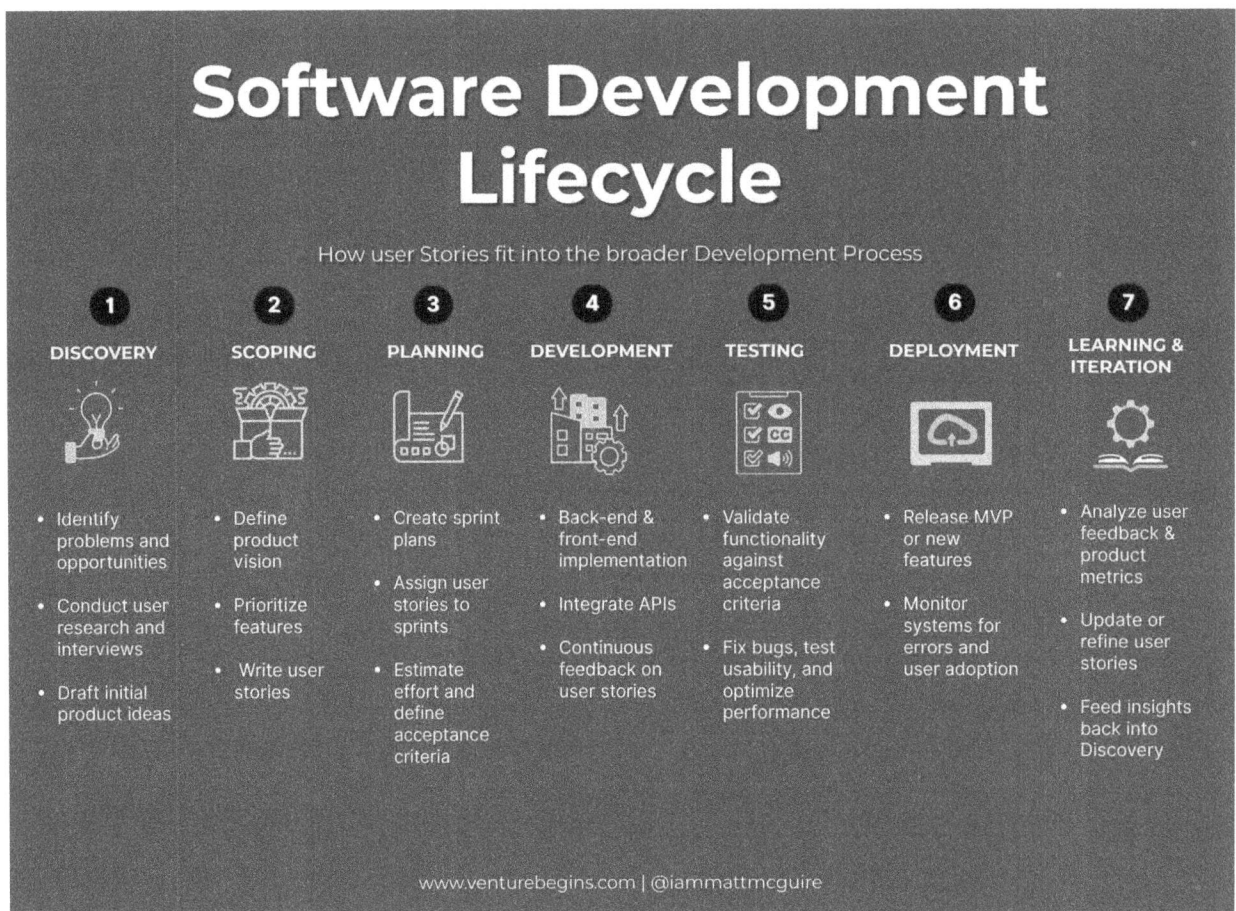

Software Development Lifecycle

How user Stories fit into the broader Development Process

1 DISCOVERY	2 SCOPING	3 PLANNING	4 DEVELOPMENT	5 TESTING	6 DEPLOYMENT	7 LEARNING & ITERATION
• Identify problems and opportunities	• Define product vision	• Create sprint plans	• Back-end & front-end implementation	• Validate functionality against acceptance criteria	• Release MVP or new features	• Analyze user feedback & product metrics
• Conduct user research and interviews	• Prioritize features	• Assign user stories to sprints	• Integrate APIs	• Fix bugs, test usability, and optimize performance	• Monitor systems for errors and user adoption	• Update or refine user stories
• Draft initial product ideas	• Write user stories	• Estimate effort and define acceptance criteria	• Continuous feedback on user stories			• Feed insights back into Discovery

www.venturebegins.com | @iammattmcguire

This guide will focus on the one thing that I've seen deliver the highest impact in the shortest amount of time. This one thing spans scoping, planning, development, and testing. You may be in disbelief, but believe me: Through trial and error, writing a great user story can make the difference between achieving alignment for your team, building a quality and reliable product, and accelerating development. The

The Founder's Guide to Technical Requirements

benefits of having this? Get to market faster than your competitors, maintain measurable consistency to set realistic and achievable development timelines, and instill confidence in your current and future investors. If you can write stellar user stories, not only will your engineers and technical team come to love you, but you'll have a rock-solid foundation upon which to build.

The first half of this document will detail what a User Story is, the template I use, some different product nomenclature where you might encounter the term, and details of the different components of a user story.

The second half of this document provides a practical example. We'll create a Products page for inventory management software. We'll have requirements, designs, and user stories so you can see them in action!

Skip to **Let's Build** if you want to get straight to the practical use and skip the background.

What is a User Story

A User Story is a prescribed **requirement** for developers or engineers to complete a specific task or tasks. It is a request for a task to be completed, not prescribing how the task should be done. User Stories should be as thorough as possible. Since they are a **requirement**, they are written with the intent that they will encompass the entirety of the requested functionality that is being asked to be developed. We want engineers to have the input of a User Story and within that, have all the information that is required to complete a task.

ENSURE YOU'RE NOT BURNING CASH

Writing incomplete requirements and *User Stories* can cause developers or engineers to come back to you with questions time and again, thus interrupting their efficiency and flow state, ultimately resulting in development delays. This time back and forth clarifying requirements and the details of a *User Story* while the developer, or engineer, is actively in development attributes to a **Sunk Development Cost** and lost efficiency.

*Want to increase efficiency and minimize **Sunk Development Costs**?*

Review the requirements and the *User Story* with the developer or engineer before development. Modify the story together to ensure alignment so that the developer or engineer can work as efficiently as possible.

Core Template Structure for a User Story / Development Task

User Story: As a [user type], I want [capability] so that [benefit].

Story Goal: [Specific outcome this feature should achieve]

Design Specification: [How the product should look - reference to designs]

Logic Specification: [How functionality should behave, data flows, storage requirements]

Acceptance Criteria:

1. [Specific condition that must be met]

2. [Another specific condition that must be met]

3. [etc.]

User Story Components

A well-structured User Story provides clear direction for Development

USER STORY

As a [type of user], I want to [perform an action] so that [achieve a goal].

Captures **who** the user is, **what** and **why** they want it.

STORY GOAL

Clear articulation of the intended business or user outcome.

Aligns the story with **value creation** and **product goals**

DESIGN SPECIFICATION

Outlines UI/UX expectations - layout, interactions, and visual behavior.

Provides **designers and developers** with **visual and interactive context**

LOGIC SPECIFICATION

Describes underlying logic, validations, and behavior rules.

Supports **backend and frontend** integrations with **technical clarity**

ACCEPTANCE CRITERIA

List of clear, testable and conditions to confirm completion.

Sets **shared understanding** of "**done**" between stakeholders

www.venturebegins.com | @iammattmcguire

Context for User Stories

The term *User Story* may be confusing. Depending on who you ask, a *User Story* may refer to the following:

- A requirement in a Product Requirements Document (PRD).

A Product Requirements Document (PRD), or another more familiar term for it may be a Business Case, is a document that details at a high-level the functionality that is proposed for development including proposed timeline, budget, and success metrics.

- A requirement belonging to an Epic.

An Epic is a term used by development teams to reference a large feature or functionality that will continually be iterated on. One or more Epics may belong in a Product Requirements Document. There is a one : many relationship between Epics and User Stories.

- A development task.

A development task is a request for a specific feature or functionality to be developed. Several development tasks are required in the development of a feature or functionality. **Example:**

  - User Story: As an inventory manager, I want to create a new product so that I can keep up to date with inventory levels.

    o Development task: [Front End] Create new Product UI

    o Dev task: [Front End] Create new Product API integration

    o Dev task: [Back End] "Create new Product" data table

    o Dev task: [Back End] "Create new Product" API

In this example, some times a *User Story* may be interchanged with a Development Task.

- The user story component of a development task. See above.

Here is a hierarchy to break it all down:

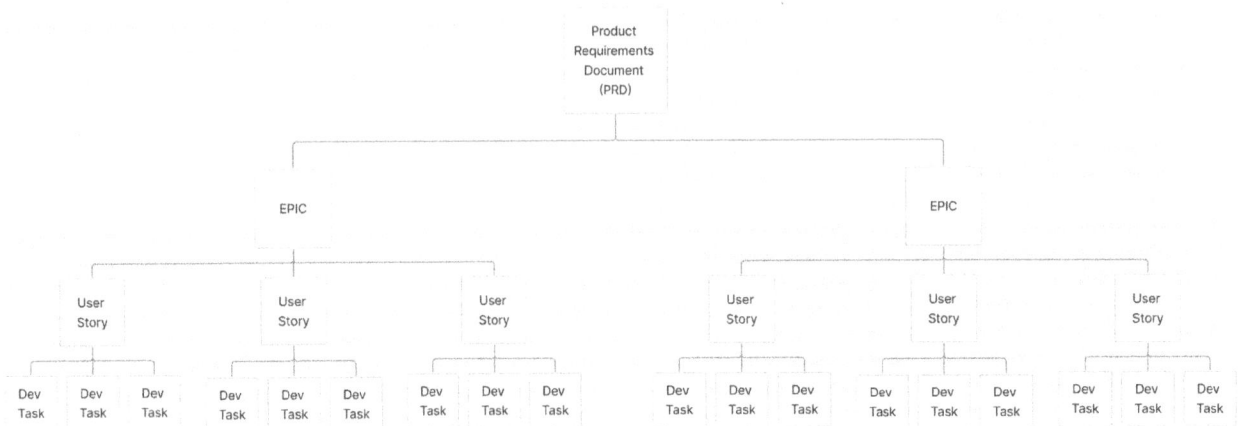

GAME CHANGING MOVE

Before proceeding in a conversation with developers, be sure to clarify with your development team: "When you use the term *User Story*, are you referring to a *User Story* that encompasses several development tasks or a specific development task?" Not only can clarifying the difference save you the headache of making the assumption but it can accelerate the working relationship with the development team.

Key Components of a User Story

Before we dive into examples, let's understand the essential elements of a well-structured user story:

User Story

- **What it is:** A simple statement that captures who wants what and why, following the format: "As a [user type], I want [capability] so that [benefit]."

- **Why it matters:** This format ensures you're focusing on the user's needs rather than just building features. It connects capabilities to specific benefits, helping prioritize what truly adds value.

- **Example:** "As an inventory manager, I want to search for products by name so that I can quickly find specific items without scrolling through the entire catalog."

The Founder's Guide to Technical Requirements

Story Goal

- **What it is:** A clear statement of the specific outcome this story/requirement/task should achieve for the business or end user.

- **Why it matters:** The goal helps everyone understand the purpose beyond just the technical implementation. It provides context for why this feature matters to your product's success.

- **Example:** "Users can find products instantly, reducing time spent on inventory management and improving operational efficiency."

Design Specification

- **What it is:** Details about the visual and interactive elements of the feature, including layout, colors, typography, and user interface components.

- **Why it matters:** Design specifications ensure the feature not only functions correctly but also presents a consistent, intuitive user experience aligned with your product's design system.

- **Example:** "The search field appears prominently at the top of the products table, with a magnifying glass icon on the right. It uses the standard text input style from our design system with placeholder text 'Search products...'"

Logic Specification

- **What it is:** Description of how the feature should behave functionally, including data flows, business rules, conditional behaviors, and technical requirements.

- **Why it matters:** Logic specifications detail the "behind the scenes" functionality that makes the feature work, ensuring developers understand all requirements beyond just the visual implementation.

- **Example:** "The search should trigger after the user stops typing for 300ms. It should query both product names and SKUs, returning partial matches. Results should only include products with available inventory."

Acceptance Criteria

- **What it is:** A list of specific, testable conditions that must be satisfied for the story to be considered complete.

- **Why it matters:** Acceptance criteria provide a clear definition of "done" that removes ambiguity and serves as a checklist during development and testing.

- **Example:**

    ○ Search returns results that match partial product names

    ○ Results appear within 200ms of user finishing typing

    ○ Empty search field shows all products

    ○ "No results found" message appears when search has zero matches

    ○ Search is not case-sensitive

Let's Build

It's one thing to talk about theory, but I've always found it most helpful to walk through a practical example. Introducing, Inventory Software. Inventory Software helps you manage and update your Inventory, simple enough.

Let's create a page that helps us to keep track of our existing products in our inventory. We want to navigate to the page, view all products in stock, search for all products in stock, and create new products. We're going to break this down into User Stories/Development tasks (I'm using the nomenclature where development task is interchangeable with user story). This functionality requires both back end data storage and front end user interfaces — that means back end and front end tasks. In order to facilitate the front end tasks, we need designs. And in order to get designs, we need to tell the designer what we're looking for, also known as requirements.

Requirements

We're going to keep these very high-level. If we were writing a Product Requirements Document, we'd have a whole lot more information regarding the product as a whole, what we're building, why we're building it, and what goals and metrics would indicate a successful outcome. That's a document for another day…

These will suffice for some back of the napkin work to get us started:

- I navigate to the page by selecting the menu item, **Products**.

- I see a table displayed of all in stock items, including:

  - Product Name

  - Assortment (which group the product belongs to)

  - The price of the product

o   How many products remain in stock

- I'm able to search all products in stock

- I can create a product.

User Stories as Requirements

Depending on the designer you work with and the working relationship that you have, they might request to have the requirements formatted as *User Stories*.

Your turn:

Given what we've learned so far and the straight forward requirements we have above, give it a shot on your own! Once you're done or you get stuck, check out mine below.

Hint: more than one straight-forward requirement can fit into a user story.

User Stories for Design

User story:

- As an inventory manager, I want to view the products page, so that I can see up to date information about our products in stock.

- **Requirements covered:**

    o   I navigate to the page by selecting the menu item, **Products**.

    o   I see a table displayed of all in stock items, including:

        ▪ Product Name

        ▪ Assortment (which group the product belongs to)

        ▪ The price of the product

        ▪ How many products remain in stock

- As an inventory manager, I want to search for an in stock product so that I can find it quickly and not scroll through a ton of pages.

- **Requirements covered:**

  - I'm able to search all products in stock

User Story

- As an inventory manager, I want to create new products so that I can digitally keep track of my inventory.

- **Requirements covered:**

  - I can create a product.

Designs

Before we build we have to understand what we're building. We're not just going to ask our developers to build the above, we need to provide them with what we want the functionality to look like.

FOR ILLUSTRATIVE PURPOSES ONLY

For the sake of time, I created some illustrative low fidelity wireframes. If you're actually developing software, you'll work with a designer to bring these to high-fidelity and have pixel dimensions. Do not give a developer or engineer this quality of design unless you have an established working relationship.

Products Page

Inventory Software			

Orders

Assortments

Products

Search   Create new product

Name	Assortment	Price	In Stock
Product 1	Blue	1.00	27
Product 2	Yellow	1.00	19
Product 3	Red	1.00	34
Product 4	White	1.00	12
Product 5	Blue	2.00	54
Product 6	Yellow	2.00	38
Product 7	Red	2.00	68
Product 8	White	2.00	24

We'd like to create a Products Page. It may look simple but there's a lot going on here. This is going to be where most of the heavy lifting is. You may be thinking: "How? It's only a search bar, table, and button. Looks pretty simple." Have you thought about the back end yet? I'll get to that in a minute.

Create new product

When you select the **_Create new product_** button, we want to deploy a modal (technical term for a pop-up) for the user to input the new product information.

Inventory Software			

Orders

Assortments

Products

Search   Create new product

Create New Product   X

Na			tock
Prod	Name:		7
Prod	Assortment:		9
Prod			4
Prod	Price:		2
Prod	In Stock:		4
Prod		Create product	8
Product 7	Red	2.00	68
Product 8	White	2.00	24

We need to ensure that all information is input into each field and there is validation (you don't want someone to put "banana" for a price). We also want to ensure we aren't overcomplicating development, so when a user selects the **X** on the modal, we want to dismiss it and disregard the data. This is okay because this maintains a user experience that is familiar for the user.

Inventory Software

Orders	Search	Create new product
Assortments		X
Products	Na	**Create New Product**	tock

	Prod	Name:	Product 9	7
	Prod	Assortment:	Red	9
	Prod			4
	Prod	Price:	3.00	2
	Prod	In Stock:	100	4
	Prod		Create product	8
	Product 7	Red	2.00	68
	Product 8	White	2.00	24

Once all the fields have the appropriate data and meet the validation criteria, we want to add the record to the database and have it displayed on the table.

Inventory Software

| Orders | Search | | Create new product |

Products

Name	Assortment	Price	In Stock
Product 1	Blue	1.00	27
Product 2	Yellow	1.00	19
Product 3	Red	1.00	34
Product 4	White	1.00	12
Product 5	Blue	2.00	54
Product 6	Yellow	2.00	38
Product 7	Red	2.00	68
Product 8	White	2.00	24
Product 9	Red	3.00	100

Pulse check

Let's look at what we've done so far..

1. We've written straight-forward requirements.

2. We've modified those straight-forward requirements as User Stories to give context to the requirements.

3. We have designs.

Front End Development

Now, it may seem like we have everything we need. BUT we're only half way there. What we've done so far has been primarily on the Front end. Front end is straightforward and can be intuitive to understand — it mainly details the user interface and user experience.

Back End Development

Now we need a way to store the data in a database and make sure that the user interface can display and interact with that stored data.

If you are thinking to yourself "Oh sh*t. I have no idea how to write or address back end. **Do not panic!**" That's what we're here to help out with. You will see the output of back end tasks through the display of data on the user interface. So while there might not be any buttons, text fields, etc. think of back end tasks as the data and information that you want to be displayed to the user and the user to interact with.

Here are some guidelines to help out with writing back end tasks.

1. **When in doubt, ask an engineer.**

2. When ever creating some new information or data in a product it will need to be stored. This is called a data structure or table.

3. If one piece of data has a relationship with another piece of data (i.e. a product belongs to an assortment. that's a relationship) then there will need to be a join.

4. In most cases, there is a middle layer between the front end user interface and the back end data structures. This is called an API. The API sends the data from the data structures to be consumed by the front end so that end users can interact with the data. An API has four functions relating to data: Create, Read, Update, and Delete (CRUD).

When in doubt, ask an engineer.

Remember, a User Story is a request for a piece of functionality to be built, not prescribe specifically how to build it.

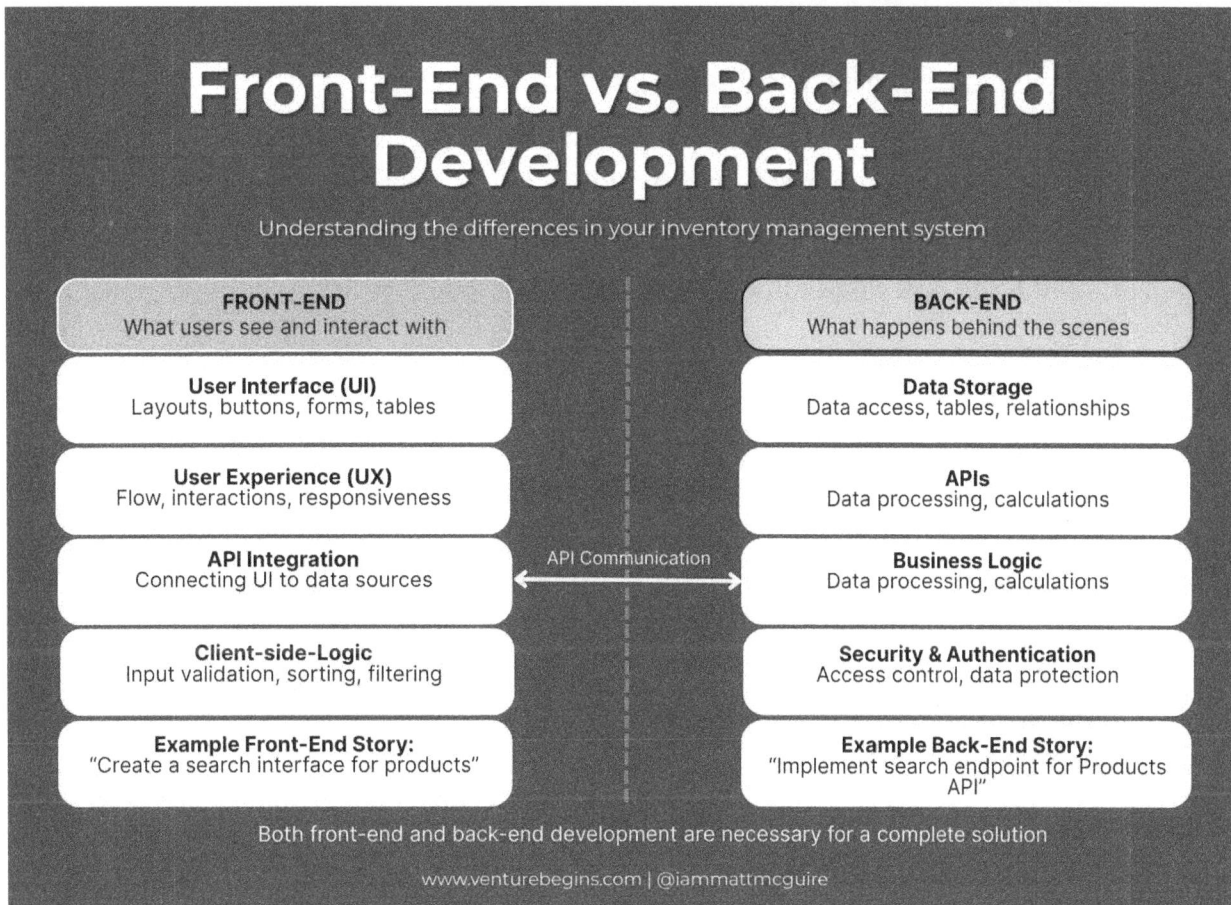

Front-End vs. Back-End Development

Understanding the differences in your inventory management system

FRONT-END	BACK-END
What users see and interact with	**What happens behind the scenes**
User Interface (UI) Layouts, buttons, forms, tables	**Data Storage** Data access, tables, relationships
User Experience (UX) Flow, interactions, responsiveness	**APIs** Data processing, calculations
API Integration Connecting UI to data sources	**Business Logic** Data processing, calculations
Client-side-Logic Input validation, sorting, filtering	**Security & Authentication** Access control, data protection
Example Front-End Story: "Create a search interface for products"	**Example Back-End Story:** "Implement search endpoint for Products API"

API Communication ←→

Both front-end and back-end development are necessary for a complete solution

www.venturebegins.com | @iammattmcguire

Development Strategy

Let's think through how to build this. Thinking through the development strategy will determine the order in which we write the User Stories.

ORDER OF OPERATIONS

Back end tasks always should be completed before front end tasks. **Back end is a dependency for front end.** The back end creates and stores the data and information displayed on the User Interface (built on the front end). If there is no data to display, what will be displayed?

Regardless of the stage of the company, business or software, if you are building new functionality, you should first build and only release the core functionality, also known as following MVP or Minimum Viable Product development. This maximizes the return on investment (ROI) timeline. You spend time developing the product, and you want to have users realize value as quickly as possible. By following this process you are also able to:

1. You are maximizing your Time To User Value (TTUV): the ratio of development investment to user realized value in a product release.

2. You are releasing functionality quickly, and getting to market fast.

3. You will be able to receive feedback on the release quickly in order to inform future development.

    3.1 Both quantitative engagement data and user feedback qualitative data.

        3.1.1 Quantitative data = how do they act

        3.1.2 Qualitative data = how do they feel

4. You are seeing a faster ROI than if you were to over extend your development team.

    4.1 Think of this scenario: you build a product with all the bells and whistles, then you release and find out that users aren't engaging with half of the functionality that your team spent the past six weeks developing. You just burned that cash.

ENSURE SUCCESS BEFORE DEVELOPMENT

The above is not an uncommon scenario. One way to mitigate the risk of poor user reception before the development investment is to validate the concept with users prior to development.

How do you do this?

Create clickable prototypes out of the designs and have a select group of existing users walk through it to understand what resonates with them, where they might get stuck or fumble, and areas that they identify the most value.

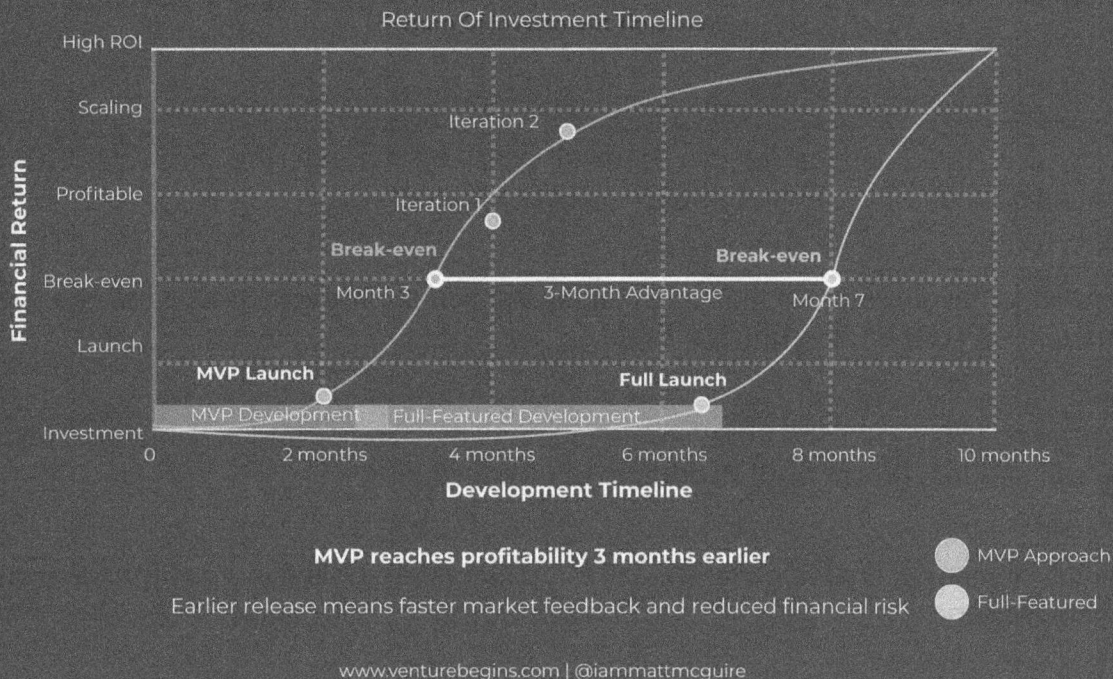

MVP vs. Full-Featured Development

Return Of Investment Timeline

MVP reaches profitability 3 months earlier

Earlier release means faster market feedback and reduced financial risk

www.venturebegins.com | @iammattmcguire

Back to the Development strategy:

First are back end tasks. Think through it logically:

1. We need a place to store the data: **[Back end] Establish a Data Structure to store Products**

2. We need to establish a relationship between assortments and products. This should be a one : many relationship — there are many products that belong to one assortment. We need to establish this early because we will be building on top of this relationship in order to display the data to the front end: **[Back end] Establish a Product-Assortment Relationship**

3. We need a way to display the data stored in the database on the user interface. As mentioned, this is done with an API:

[Back end] Establish Products API Development

We now have all the back end pieces in place in order to display data on the user interface. Now, we don't want to overwhelm the developer and ask for too much at once. The more we ask for in a single User Story, the more likely something is going to get missed. Think of going to the grocery store with a list of three things to get vs a list three pages long.

4. We need a user interface for the users to view and manage the products. This is the frame surrounding the picture: **[Front end] Products Page UI**

5. We need to have a table on the UI to display the actual Products that are stored in the database to the user: **[Front end] Products Table**

6. Once we build the UI of the table, we need to ensure it is appropriately mapped and displays the data as intended: **[Front end] Products API Integration**

7. Limit the number of products that we ask for at once through pagination: **[Front end] Pagination Implementation**

   Why do we need this?

   Picture you're at a restaurant and you ask for 10 breadsticks. No big deal, a server can deliver that in one trip. Now imagine if you asked for 1,000 bread sticks — no way that server is going to be able to deliver all 1,000 in one trip, it's going to take them a while. It's the same case for displaying data! The wait we encounter is what we refer to as latency.

8. Finally, we need to be able to create new products through the user interface: **[Front end] Create Product Modal**

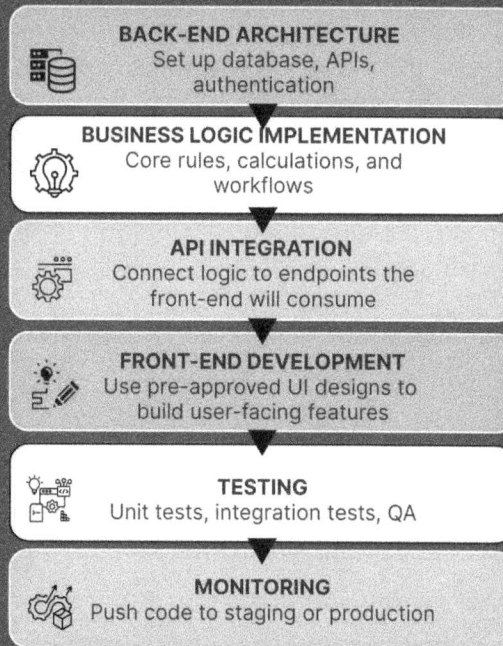

Development Process Chart

Key Principle: Back-end is a dependency for front-end

BACK-END ARCHITECTURE
Set up database, APIs, authentication

BUSINESS LOGIC IMPLEMENTATION
Core rules, calculations, and workflows

API INTEGRATION
Connect logic to endpoints the front-end will consume

FRONT-END DEVELOPMENT
Use pre-approved UI designs to build user-facing features

TESTING
Unit tests, integration tests, QA

MONITORING
Push code to staging or production

www.venturebegins.com | @iammattmcguire

Inventory Software User Stories

Alright! We finally have everything we need. Let's write these User Stories. To help understand which User Stories are required for each step, I'm going to show which User Stories are required to develop each UI and the order in which they should be built.

Products Page

Inventory Software			

Orders	Search		Create new product
Assortments			
Products			

Name	Assortment	Price	In Stock
Product 1	Blue	1.00	27
Product 2	Yellow	1.00	19
Product 3	Red	1.00	34
Product 4	White	1.00	12
Product 5	Blue	2.00	54
Product 6	Yellow	2.00	38
Product 7	Red	2.00	68
Product 8	White	2.00	24

1. [Back end] Establish a Data Structure to store Products

User Story:

As an inventory manager, I want to view the products page, so that I can see up to date information about our products in stock.

Story Goal:

A data storage system exists that can reliably store all product information and maintain connections between products and their assortments.

Design Specification:

N/A

Logic Specification:

Create a system to store product data including ID, Name, Assortment, Price, and In Stock quantity. Ensure products are properly connected to their assortments.

Acceptance Criteria:

1. Product information can be stored with all required fields.

2. Each product has a unique identifier.

3. Products are correctly linked to their assortments.

4. The system can handle all basic data operations (create, read, update, delete).

5. The system records when products are created or modified.

Key Insights:

- The acceptance criteria clearly define what "done" means for this task

- Notice how this story doesn't specify implementation details like database type or schema design

2. [Back end] Establish a Product-Assortment Relationship

User Story:

As an inventory manager, I want to view the products page, so that I can see up to date information about our products in stock.

Story Goal:

Products and assortments are linked in the system, allowing users to organize and filter products by their assortment categories.

Design Specification:

N/A

Logic Specification:

Implement a connection between products and assortments. Ensure this connection maintains data integrity.

Acceptance Criteria:

1. Products can be assigned to specific assortments.

2. The system prevents deletion of assortments that have products assigned to them.

3. Products can be easily found by their assortment.

4. When viewing a product, its assortment information is available.

5. The system handles these connections efficiently.

Key Insights:

- This story focuses on a specific relationship between two data entities

- The acceptance criteria address data integrity constraints

- This illustrates how even backend tasks should focus on user-facing outcomes

3. [Back end] Establish Products API Development

User Story:

As an inventory manager, I want to view the products page, so that I can see up to date information about our products in stock.

Story Goal:

A complete set of backend services exists that enables all necessary product data operations with proper validation and error handling.

Design Specification:

N/A

Logic Specification:

Develop services that allow listing, creating, retrieving, updating, and deleting products. Include features for pagination, sorting, and filtering. Ensure proper data validation and error handling.

Acceptance Criteria:

1. The system can retrieve a list of products with pagination.

2. New products can be created with proper validation.

3. Individual products can be retrieved, updated, and deleted.

4. The system handles errors appropriately and provides helpful messages.

5. The services support sorting and filtering of products.

Key Insights:

- API development stories should clearly define all required endpoints and operations

- Error handling requirements are explicitly included

- Performance considerations like pagination are addressed upfront

4. [Front end] Products Page UI

User Story:

As an inventory manager, I want to view the products page, so that I can see up to date information about our products in stock.

Story Goal:

Users can navigate to a visually coherent Products page with all necessary UI components properly positioned and styled according to design specifications.

Design Specification:

Create a page with a menu bar at the top, product list in the center, search bar above the list, and "Create new product" button above the list. The Products menu item should be highlighted in orange and bold when selected.

[link to Figma or other tool design file]

Logic Specification:

Implement the basic page layout with proper component structure. Ensure the Products menu item remains in active state until another menu item is selected.

Acceptance Criteria:

1. Page layout matches the design specification.

2. Products menu item is highlighted in orange and bold when selected.

3. Layout is responsive and maintains proper alignment across different screen sizes.

4. Visual styling adheres to the application's design system.

5. Menu item remains in active state until another menu item is selected.

Key Insights:

- Design specifications include specific UI details like colors and states

- Responsive design requirements are included

- This story focuses on the layout structure without implementation of functional components

5. [Front end] Products Table

User Story:

As an inventory manager, I want a clear table view of products so that I can easily scan and analyze my inventory.

Story Goal:

Users can view product data in a visually organized table with alternating row colors, clear column headers, and appropriate pagination.

Design Specification:

Create a table with alternating row colors (light blue #56a0d3 and white #FFFFFF). Display columns for Name, Assortment, Price, and "In Stock". Limit display to 10 items per page.

[link to Figma or other tool design file]

Logic Specification:

Implement a table component that displays product data with appropriate styling. Enable column header clicking for sorting functionality. Implement client-side paging if needed.

Acceptance Criteria:

1. Table displays product data with alternating row colors.

2. Table shows Name, Assortment, Price, and "In Stock" columns.

3. Table is limited to 10 items per page.

4. Column headers are clickable for sorting.

5. Table updates correctly when data changes.

Key Insights:

- Specific design details like exact color codes are included

- The story focuses on one component (the table) rather than the entire page

- Both visual and behavioral requirements are defined

6. [Front end] Products API Integration

User Story:

As an inventory manager, I want to view the products page, so that I can see up to date information about our products in stock.

Story Goal:

All front-end components are connected to the appropriate backend services, with proper data flow, error handling, and loading states.

Design Specification:

N/A

Logic Specification:

Implement service functions to call the product management services. Handle responses and error states. Update UI components to use real data instead of mock data.

Acceptance Criteria:

1. Product list loads data from the backend services.

2. Sorting and pagination work correctly with the backend.

3. Search functionality connects to the search service.

4. Creating a new product successfully saves to the backend and updates the UI.

5. Error handling is implemented for service failures.

6. Loading states are shown during backend calls.

Key Insights:

- This integration story connects previously completed frontend and backend components

- Loading states and error handling are explicitly required

- The focus is on real data flow rather than visual design

7. [Front end] Pagination Implementation

User Story:

As an inventory manager, I want to view the products page, so that I can see up to date information about our products in stock.

Story Goal:

Users can navigate through multiple pages of products when more than 10 items exist, with clear indication of current page and total pages.

Design Specification:

Create pagination controls below the products table.

[link to Figma or other tool design file]

Logic Specification:

Implement pagination controls that interact with the backend pagination. Display current page, total pages, and navigation buttons.

Acceptance Criteria:

1. Pagination controls appear when there are more than 10 products.

2. Current page is visually indicated.

3. Clicking navigation buttons loads the appropriate page of products.

4. Pagination state is maintained when sorting or filtering products.

5. Pagination controls are disabled appropriately when at first or last page.

Key Insights:

- Edge cases (disabling controls at first/last page) are addressed

- State persistence requirements (maintaining pagination during sorting) are specified

- The story focuses on a specific UI component that enhances usability

Create a Product

Inventory Software

Orders	Search			Create new product
Assortments		**Create New Product**	X	
Products	Na			:ock
	Prod	Name:		7
	Prod	Assortment:		9
	Prod			4
	Prod	Price:		2
	Prod	In Stock:		4
	Prod			8
			Create product	
	Product 7	Red	2.00	68
	Product 8	White	2.00	24

Inventory Software

Orders	Search			Create new product
Assortments		**Create New Product**	X	
Products	Na			:ock
	Prod	Name:	Product 9	7
	Prod	Assortment:	Red	9
	Prod			4
	Prod	Price:	3.00	2
	Prod	In Stock:	100	4
	Prod			8
			Create product	
	Product 7	Red	2.00	68
	Product 8	White	2.00	24

Inventory Software

Orders	Search			Create new product
Assortments				
Products	Name	Assortment	Price	In Stock
	Product 1	Blue	1.00	27
	Product 2	Yellow	1.00	19
	Product 3	Red	1.00	34
	Product 4	White	1.00	12
	Product 5	Blue	2.00	54
	Product 6	Yellow	2.00	38
	Product 7	Red	2.00	68
	Product 8	White	2.00	24
	Product 9	Red	3.00	100

8. [Front end] Create Product Modal

User Story:

As an inventory manager, I want to create new products so that I can digitally keep track of my inventory.

Story Goal:

Users can click a button to open a modal form, enter valid product information, and successfully create new products in the system.

Design Specification:

Create a modal with the title "Create New Product" in the top left. Include labeled fields for Name, Assortment, Price, and "In Stock". Labels should be left-aligned, and fields should be aligned 15px to the right of the longest label. Add a close button (X) in the top-right corner and a "Create Product" button in the bottom-right corner.

[link to Figma or other tool design file]

Logic Specification:

Implement a modal component with form validation: Name (alphanumeric), Assortment (alphanumeric), Price (numeric only), and In Stock (numeric only). All fields are required. On form submission, call the product creation API endpoint.

Acceptance Criteria:

1. Modal appears when "Create new product" button is clicked.

2. Form fields have appropriate validation rules.

3. "X" button closes the modal without saving.

4. "Create Product" button is enabled only when all fields are valid.

5. Form layout matches the design specification with proper alignment.

6. Error messages display appropriately for invalid inputs.

Key Insights:

- Detailed layout specifications with exact measurements

- Validation rules for each field are clearly defined

- Both success and error paths are addressed

Product Enhancements

Product enhancements are iterations to deliver additional value to your users that are beyond the minimum scope of the functionality to get it to market.

The below would be my personal recommendation but at the end of the day it's all about what's going to deliver value to the user as quickly as possible. So make sure you validate before you build!

[Back end] Search Functionality

User Story:

N/A

Story Goal:

Users can search for products and receive fast, accurate results showing only items that are currently in stock.

Design Specification:

N/A

Logic Specification:

Create a search service that finds products by name and only includes products with available stock. Optimize the search for speed and accuracy.

Acceptance Criteria:

1. The search service finds products that match the search terms.

2. Only products with stock are included in search results.

3. The search works with partial words and is not case-sensitive.

4. Search results are delivered quickly (under 200ms).

5. The search system is optimized for performance with large product catalogs.

Key Insights:

- Search functionality often warrants its own story due to complexity

- Performance requirements are explicitly stated (200ms response time) — this isn't always required to explicitly call out but is a nice to have.

- Business rules (only showing in-stock products) are clearly defined

[Front end] Search Implementation

User Story:

As an inventory manager, I want to search for an in stock product so that I can find it quickly and not scroll through a ton of pages.

Story Goal:

Users can enter search terms and see only the in-stock products that match their query, with results updating after they finish typing.

Design Specification:

Create a search text field above the products table.

[link to Figma or other tool design file]

Logic Specification:

Implement a search component that triggers a search query 2 seconds after the user stops typing. Only query products that have an "In Stock" value. Send search parameters to the API endpoint.

Acceptance Criteria:

1. Search field is properly positioned above the products table.

2. Search triggers 2 seconds after user stops typing.

3. Only products with "In Stock" values are included in search results.

4. Search results update the product list in real-time.

5. An appropriate message displays when no matching products are found.

Key Insights:

- User experience details like search timing are specified

- Business rules (only searching in-stock products) are included

- Error states (no results found) are addressed

[Front end] Products table Sorting Functionality

User Story:

As an inventory manager, I want to sort products by different properties so that I can analyze my inventory from different perspectives.

Story Goal:

Users can click on any column header to sort the products list in ascending or descending order, with a clear visual indication of the current sort order.

Design Specification:

Column headers in the products table should be clickable and indicate sort direction.

[link to Figma or other tool design file]

Logic Specification:

Implement client-side or server-side sorting functionality. The first click sorts in ascending order, and a second click sorts in descending order.

Acceptance Criteria:

1. Clicking a column header sorts data in ascending order.

2. Clicking the same header again sorts in descending order.

3. Visual indicator shows which column is being sorted and in which direction.

4. Sorting is maintained when navigating between pages.

5. Sorting state is passed correctly to API calls if server-side sorting is used.

Key Insights:

- The story allows flexibility in implementation (client-side or server-side)

- The exact behavior of sort toggling is specified

- Visual indicators for the current sort state are required

Best Practices for Writing Effective User Stories

Based on the examples above, here are some key practices to adopt when writing user stories for your startup's development projects:

1. Be Specific and Measurable

Your user stories should contain enough detail that both you and your development team have a clear understanding of what needs to be built and how to determine when it's complete. Vague requirements lead to misunderstandings and rework.

Example: Instead of "The system should be fast," specify "Search results should be delivered in under 200ms."

2. Focus on User Value

Even for technical components, try to connect the work to user or business value. This helps prioritize features and keeps the team focused on outcomes rather than just outputs.

Example: Instead of "Implement a database for products," specify "Create a product storage system so that we can save and access product information."

3. Include Clear Acceptance Criteria

Acceptance criteria provide a definitive "checklist" that determines when a story is complete. They should be specific, testable conditions that remove ambiguity.

Example: For a login feature, include criteria like "Users receive an error message when entering an incorrect password" and "Users are redirected to the dashboard after successful login."

4. Separate Design and Logic

By separating visual design specifications from functional logic, you make it easier for different specialists (designers and developers) to understand their responsibilities.

Example: Design Specification focuses on colors, layouts, and positioning, while Logic Specification addresses behavior, data flow, and error handling.

5. Address Edge Cases and Error States

Don't just focus on the "happy path" where everything works perfectly. Include requirements for handling errors, edge cases, and unexpected inputs. This prevents many common issues in production systems.

Example: Include criteria like "Appropriate message displays when no matching products are found" and "System prevents deletion of assortments that have products assigned to them."

6. Keep Stories Manageable

Break complex features into smaller, focused stories that can be completed within a single sprint or development cycle. This limits the chances for something to be missed, improves estimation accuracy and allows for more frequent delivery of value.

Example: Instead of one massive "Product Management" story, we broke it down into specific components like layout, table implementation, sorting, search, and creation functionality.

7. Use Consistent Terminology

Establish a consistent vocabulary with your development team to avoid confusion. What you call a "category" shouldn't be called an "assortment" elsewhere in your specifications.

Example: Notice how "assortment" is consistently used throughout all stories rather than switching between terms like "category" or "group."

8. Document Integration Points

Clearly specify how different components should interact with each other, particularly when they're being developed by different team members or at different times.

Example: The "API Integration" story explicitly defines how the frontend components should connect to the backend services.

Good vs. Bad User Story

A well-crafted user story speaks to real problems your users face—like stockouts that hurt revenue. It helps your team build features that solve the right problems, not just add more stuff.

ASPECT	GOOD USER STORY Provides clear direction for implementation	BAD USER STORY Leads to misunderstanding and rework
Format	As a store manager, I want to receive low-stock alerts so that I can reorder inventory in time.	Add a stock alert system.
Clarity	Clear user role, intent, and business impact	Ambiguous and lacks user perspective
Goal-Oriented	Focuses on solving a real operational problem	Focuses on a feature without context
Testable Criteria	Can be tested: "Alert appears when item falls below threshold."	Hard to validate what "add" actually means
Collaborative	Opens up discussion about thresholds, notification methods, and user roles	Leaves gaps in understanding and assumptions

www.venturebegins.com | @iammattmcguire

Why is this important

Think of building software like building a house. You wouldn't just tell a contractor, *'Build me a house'* and expect a perfect result. You'd need to define:

- How many rooms? How many floors?

- What type of kitchen would you like? What material do you prefer for counter top?

- Do you want a house that just looks good, or one that lasts for decades?

When you skip corners, you'll build on a fragile foundation and accumulate Tech Debt.

Technical Debt Illustration

Understanding the differences in your inventory management system

QUICK & HACKY APPROACH

EVENTUAL COLLAPSED
Short-term Thinking

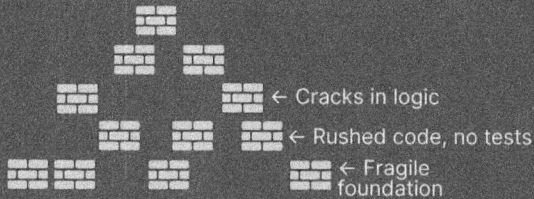

← Cracks in logic
← Rushed code, no tests
← Fragile foundation

Looks quicker short-term, but leads to hidden issues, unstable builds, and painful scaling.

Long-term Consequences:
Frequent bugs & slowdowns
More costly fixes later
Developer burnout

CLEAN & STRUCTURED APPROACH

STABLE GROWTH
Long-term Thinking

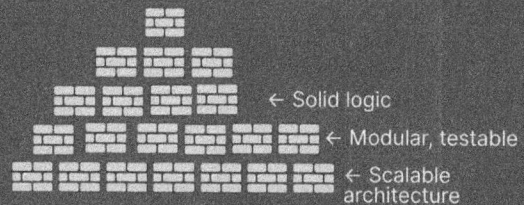

← Solid logic
← Modular, testable
← Scalable architecture

Takes more upfront effort, but the result is robust, maintainable, and future-proof.

Long-term Benefits:
Easier updates & maintenance
Lower long-term costs
Happier team & faster growth

www.venturebegins.com | @iammattmcguire

So remember, when in doubt, add detail!

Why This Approach Works for Startup Founders

As a founder focusing on building your business, you need your development team to deliver quality software efficiently. This structured approach to user stories provides several key benefits:

1. Clearer Communication

By breaking down features into well-defined stories with specific acceptance criteria, you drastically reduce misunderstandings between you and your technical team. This leads to fewer costly revisions and rework.

2. Better Prioritization

When features are broken down into discrete components, you can more easily prioritize what needs to be built first based on business value, technical dependencies, and resource constraints.

3. More Accurate Planning

Smaller, well-defined user stories allow for more accurate time and effort estimates, which improves sprint planning and roadmap reliability.

4. Increased Accountability

Clear acceptance criteria make it obvious when a story is complete, improving accountability and preventing scope creep.

5. Improved Quality

By explicitly addressing error states, edge cases, and integration points, you reduce the likelihood of defects and usability issues in your product.

6. Faster Time to Market

A structured approach allows your team to work on multiple components in parallel and deliver incremental value rather than waiting for an entire feature to be completed.

Conclusion

Effective communication is the cornerstone of successful software development. By adopting this structured approach to user stories, you're equipping your team with the clarity they need to turn your vision into reality efficiently and accurately.

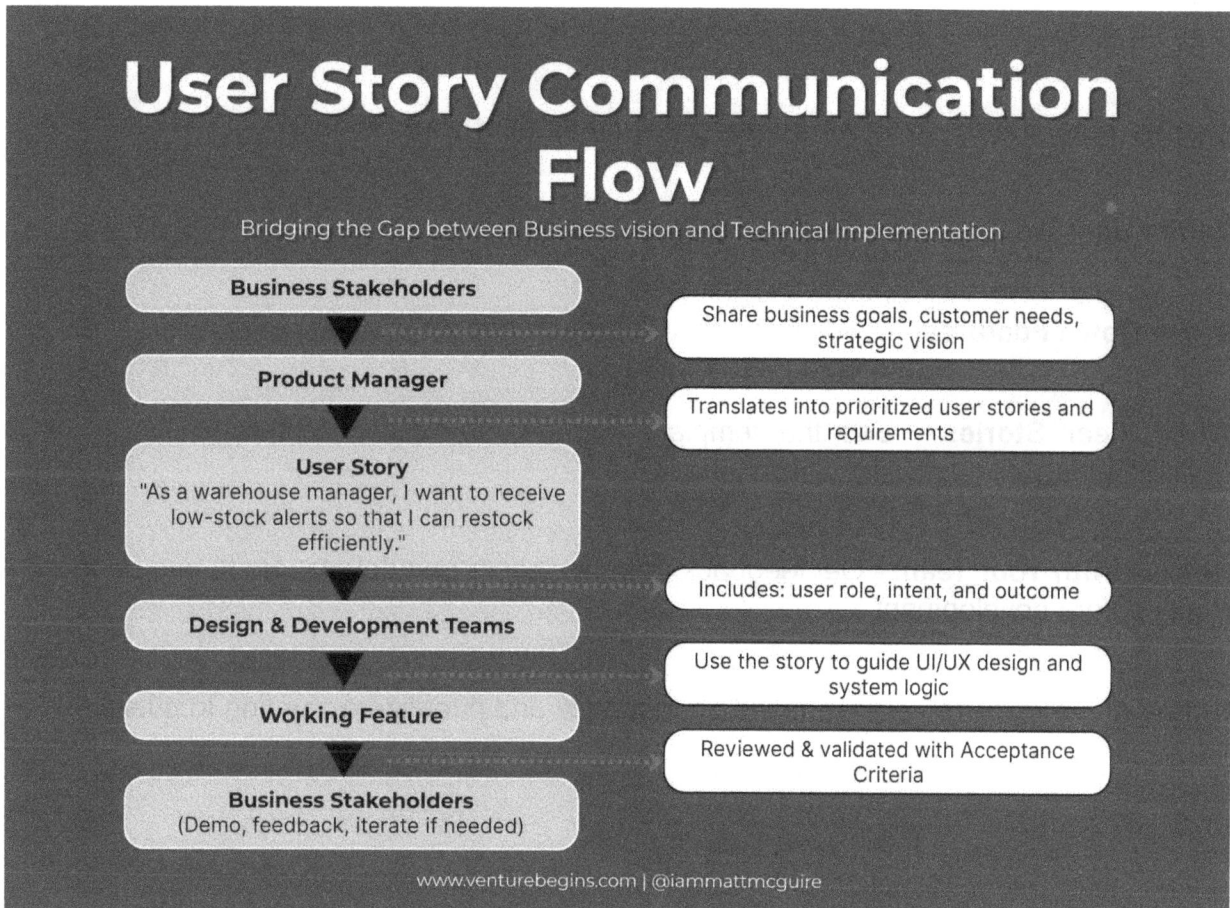

User Story Communication Flow

Bridging the Gap between Business vision and Technical Implementation

- **Business Stakeholders** → Share business goals, customer needs, strategic vision
- **Product Manager** → Translates into prioritized user stories and requirements
- **User Story** "As a warehouse manager, I want to receive low-stock alerts so that I can restock efficiently." → Includes: user role, intent, and outcome
- **Design & Development Teams** → Use the story to guide UI/UX design and system logic
- **Working Feature** → Reviewed & validated with Acceptance Criteria
- **Business Stakeholders** (Demo, feedback, iterate if needed)

www.venturebegins.com | @iammattmcguire

Remember that the goal isn't bureaucracy or excessive documentation—it's creating just enough structure to ensure everyone has a shared understanding of what needs to be built and why. This balanced approach is particularly valuable for startup founders who need to move quickly while maintaining quality and managing costs.

Getting Started with your Own User Stories

Ready to apply this approach to your startup's development process? Here's how to get started:

1. **Identify Your Users** - Who will be using each feature of your product?

2. **Define User Goals** - What are they trying to accomplish?

3. **Break Down Features** - Divide large features into manageable components

4. **Write Clear Stories** - Use the template provided to create comprehensive, unambiguous requirements

5. **Review With Your Team** - Get feedback from designers and developers to ensure feasibility and clarity before development

6. **Refine and Prioritize** - Adjust based on feedback and prioritize according to business value

How Venture Begins Can Help

As a seed or Series A founder, you know that the road to successful fundraising and scaling is paved with technical challenges that can delay your time to market and burn through your runway. At Venture Begins, we partner with founders like you to implement product operations that impress investors and enable efficient growth after funding.

The Challenges You're Facing

From my conversations with founders at your stage, I understand the frustrations you might be experiencing:

- **Technical communication gaps** that lead to misaligned expectations and delayed launches, raising red flags during investor due diligence

- **Development timelines that stretch beyond projections**, damaging investor confidence and threatening future funding rounds

- **Accumulating technical debt** that limits your ability to deploy capital efficiently post-funding

- **Inconsistent development processes** that make it difficult to demonstrate scalability to investors

- **Difficulty translating product vision** into technical requirements that development teams can execute reliably

How We Transform Your Product Operations

Our approach bridges the gap between fundraising requirements and technical execution:

Strategic Planning for Fundraising Success

- Create investor-ready roadmaps that demonstrate clear vision and execution capability

- Establish metrics that matter to Series A investors and VCs

- Align technical strategy with fundraising timelines and milestones

Development Optimization

- Implement efficient sprint processes to accelerate development by 40-60%

- Structure development workflows that demonstrate scalability to investors

- Establish governance that proves you can efficiently deploy millions in capital

Data-Driven Development

- Build analytics frameworks that provide the metrics investors demand

- Establish KPIs that directly connect product performance to business growth

- Create feedback loops that demonstrate product-market fit to potential investors

Technical Communication

- Facilitate effective communication between technical and non-technical stakeholders

- Create documentation systems that survive investor scrutiny

- Prepare technical presentations for investor meetings and due diligence

Measuring Successful Outcomes

We focus on metrics that directly impact your fundraising success and ability to scale:

- **Development predictability metrics** that build investor confidence

- **Capital efficiency indicators** that demonstrate responsible resource management

- **Technical debt measurements** that show a sustainable growth trajectory

- **Team productivity analytics** that prove your ability to scale with funding

Results Our Clients Achieve

- **Successful fundraising** with stronger technical due diligence performance

- **Faster deployment of capital** after funding rounds

- **More efficient scaling** without proportional team growth

- **Enhanced investor reporting** with clear visibility into development progress

- **Sustainable growth model** that scales from seed through Series B and beyond

Resources

To explore how we can help you overcome your specific development challenges. Book a discovery call where we'll discuss your current situation and identify the biggest opportunities for improvement.

- **Venture Begins**: To work with us directly, visit our site at venturebegins.com

- **Join our Founder Collective**: To gain access to additional resources, support, and take a seamless first step towards preparing for your Series A funding or Scale your Series A business join our community: https://www.skool.com/founders-scale-up-collective-5342

This is Not "Just Another Guide"

This is a straightforward guide. I'm not going to waste your time with fluff or theory. But before we begin, understand something important: don't take advice about building software from someone who hasn't (a) successfully built products that scale and (b) helped founders navigate technical challenges without a technical background.

I discovered this the hard way. Despite having success as a product manager at renowned companies, I found myself struggling to communicate the complex world of software development to founders who had brilliant ideas but couldn't speak "tech." The communication gap was costing them time, money, and in some cases, their entire business.

As you build your software product, you'll face critical decisions about what to prioritize, how to communicate with developers, and where to invest your limited resources. These decisions will either create a solid foundation for growth or trap you in a cycle of constant rework, technical debt, and missed deadlines.

Think of it like trying to build a house without speaking the language of architecture. Could you figure it out through trial and error? Maybe. But why spend your precious runway learning painful lessons when the blueprint for success already exists?

If your development team stopped understanding your vision today, would your product still match what your customers need tomorrow? For most founders without technical backgrounds, the answer is no.

I can't build your software for you, but I can show you how to transform your vision into clear technical requirements that developers can execute flawlessly. I've helped dozens of founders make this transition, bridging the gap between business goals and technical implementation.

Here's what you need to know: the journey from idea to successful software product doesn't have to be filled with expensive mistakes and miscommunications. Everything in this guide is about breaking free from the traditional founder-developer disconnect and giving you the tools to lead your technical team with confidence—even if you've never written a line of code.

ISBN 9798998847714

90000

9 798998 847714